THIS WALKER BOOK BELONGS TO:

_____

_____

_____

_____

For Louis

First published 1995 by Walker Books Ltd
87 Vauxhall Walk, London SE11 5HJ

This edition published 1996

10 9 8 7 6 5 4

© 1995 Flora McDonnell

This book has been typeset in New Baskerville.

Printed in Hong Kong/China

British Library Cataloguing in Publication Data
A catalogue record for this book is available
from the British Library.

ISBN 0-7445-4373-8

I Love Boats

Flora McDonnell

WALKER BOOKS
AND SUBSIDIARIES
LONDON · BOSTON · SYDNEY

I love the old boat being painted red and green.

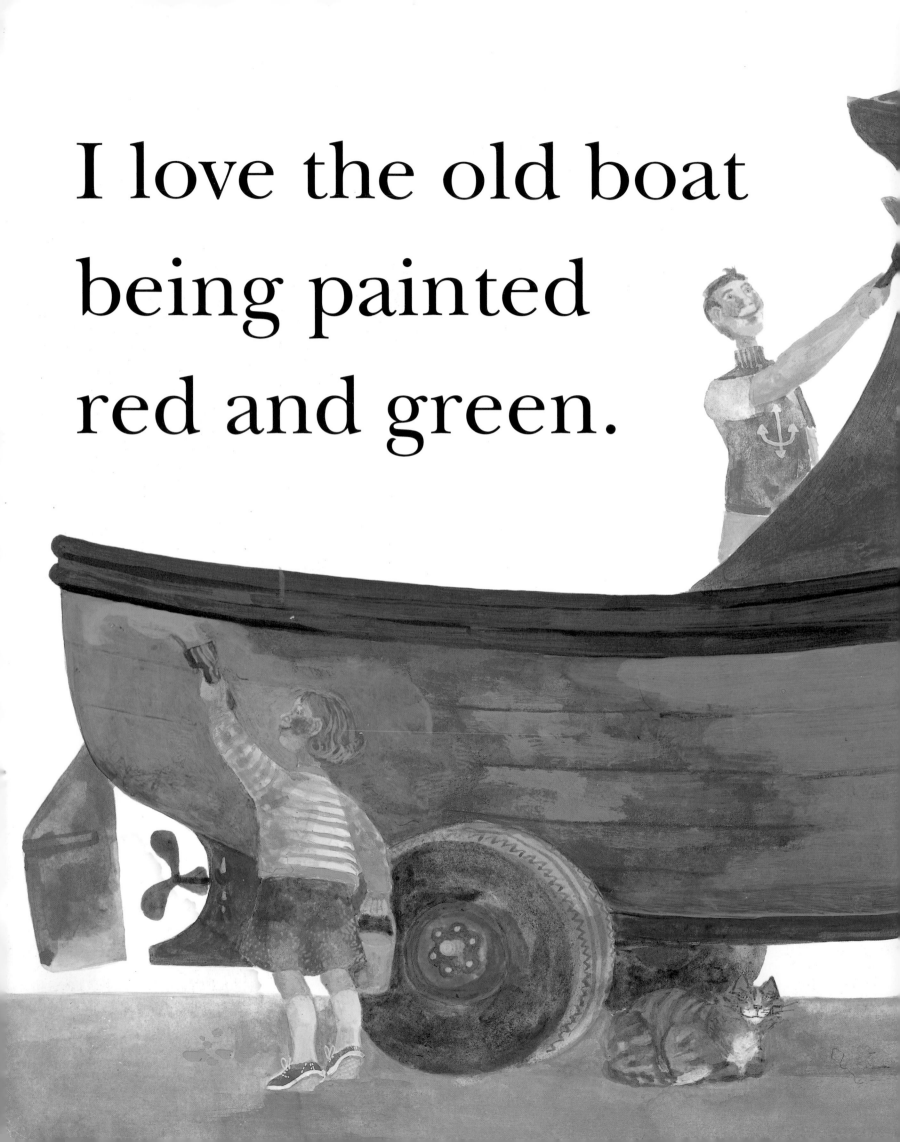

I love the houseboat

with a family on board.

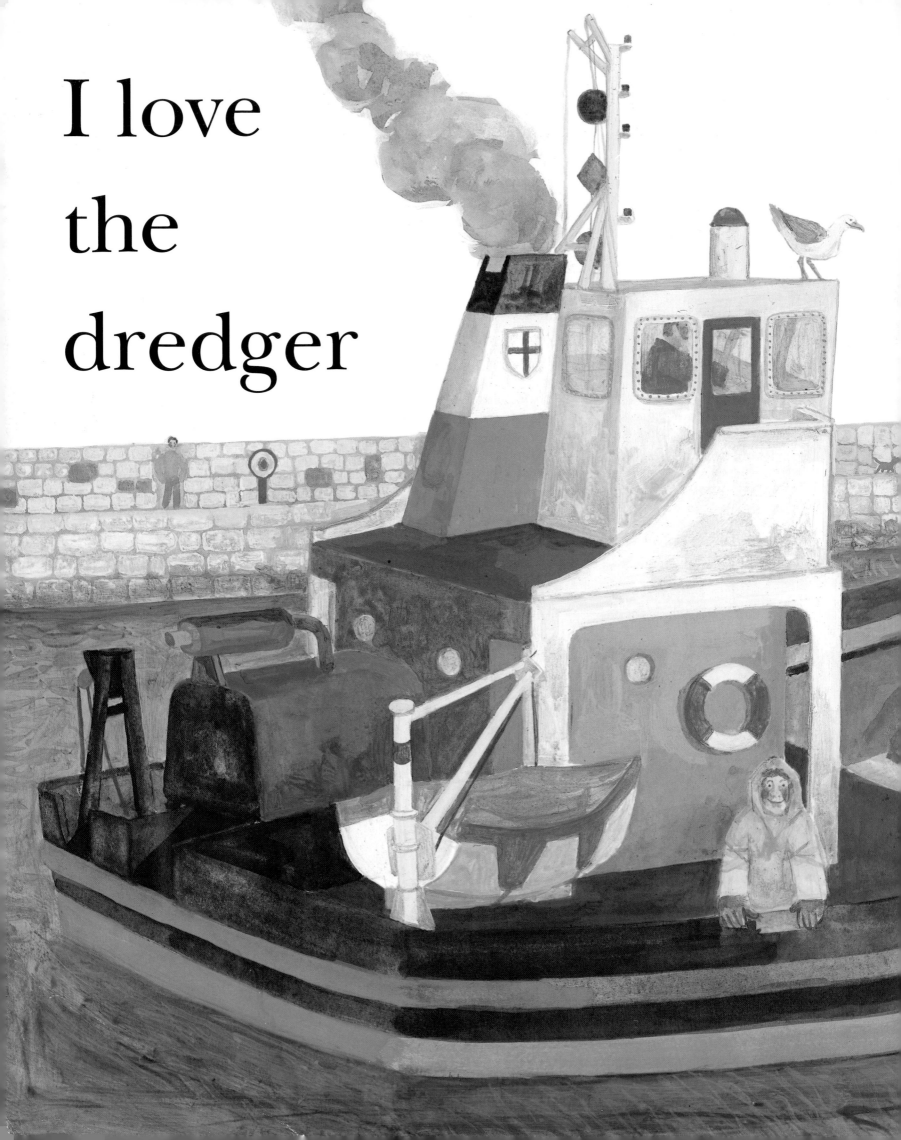

I love
the
dredger

scooping
up the
mud.

I love the
lobster potter

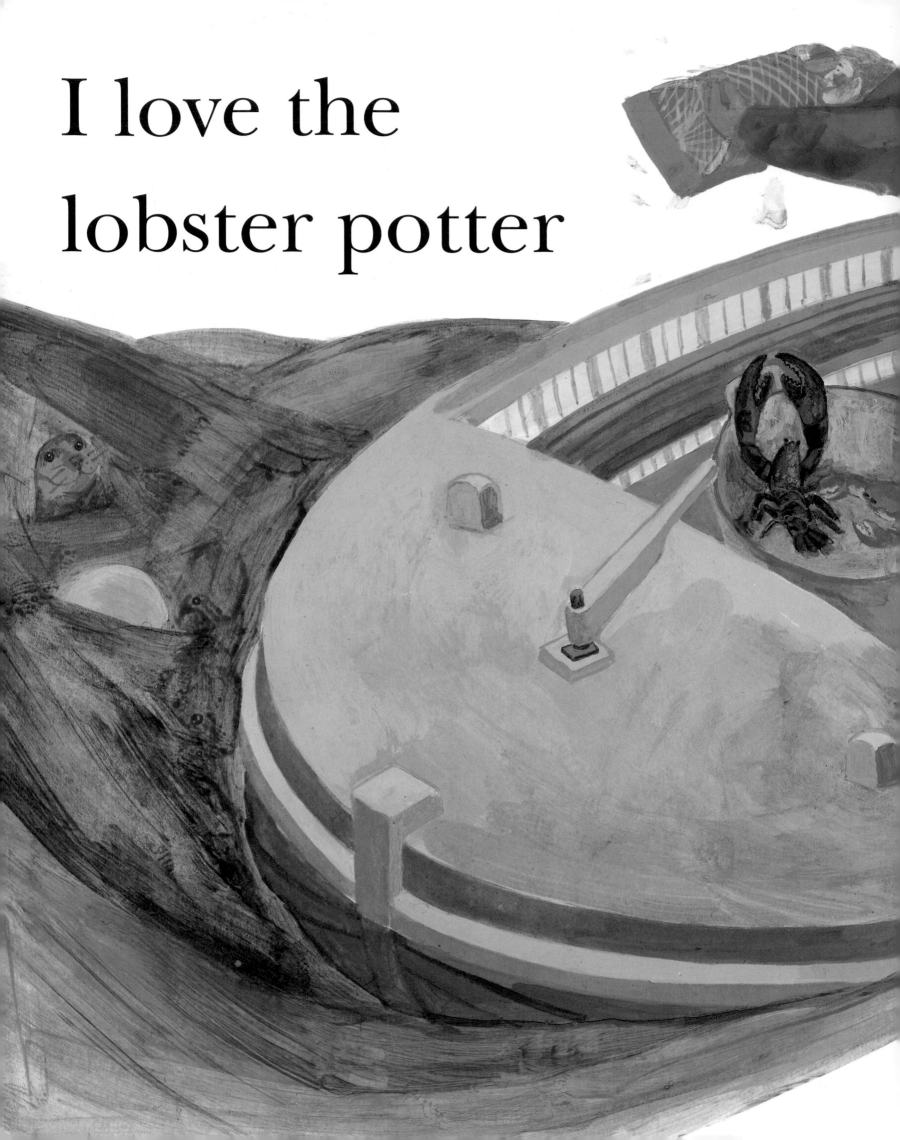

bobbing on the waves.

I love the ferry
loading up
with cars.

I love the cargo boat with lots of crates on deck.

I love the tug towing a big ship out to sea.

I love the liner
far out on the ocean.

I love the
sailing boat

speeding with the wind.

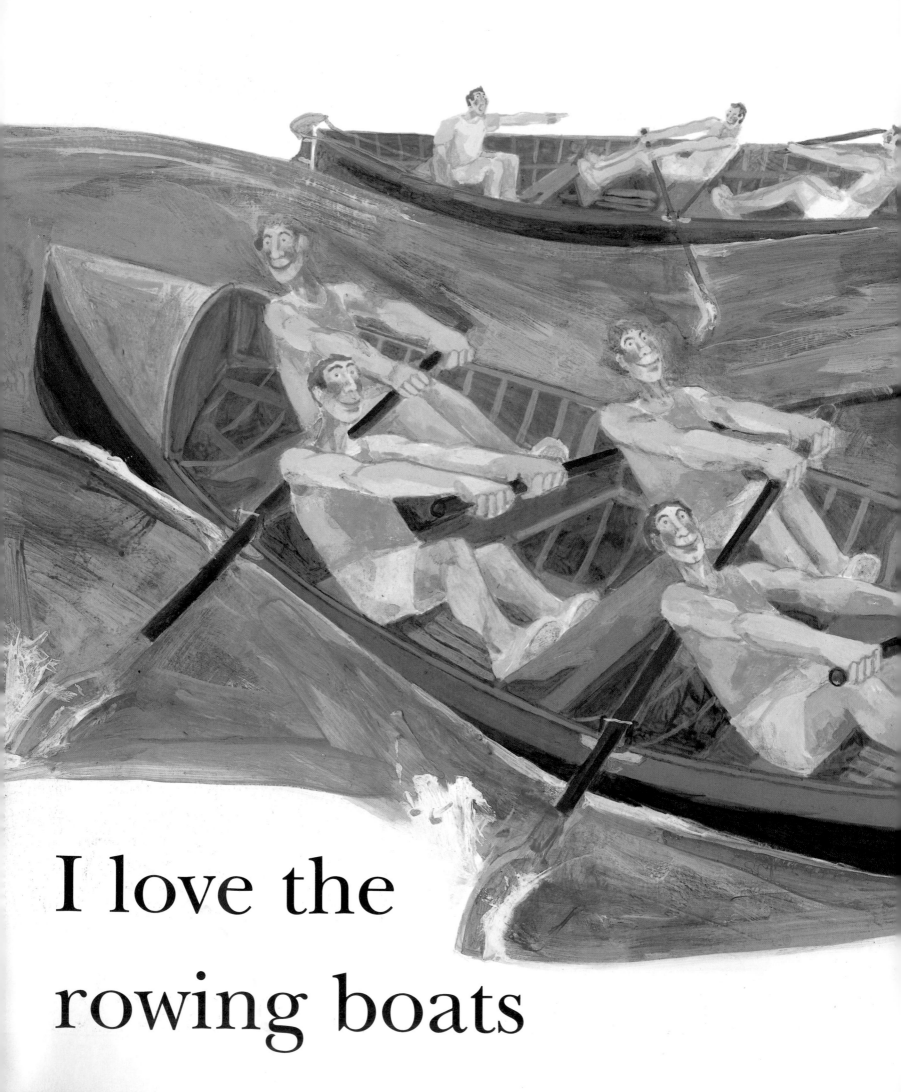

I love the
rowing boats

racing round the rock.

I love the trawlers bringing home the fish.

I love all the boats

floating in my bath.

MORE WALKER PAPERBACKS
For You to Enjoy

I LOVE ANIMALS
by Flora McDonnell

Winner of the Mother Goose Award

"Beautifully drawn animals… Guaranteed to delight any child…
A good book to start children thinking about both
words and animals." *Nursery World*

0-7445-4346-0   £5.99

FLORA McDONNELL'S ABC
by Flora McDonnell

For ABC read appealing, bold, colourful.
This big, bright alphabet book is a joy from A to Z!

"A grand way to learn letters." *The Observer*

0-7445-6007-1   £5.99

THE NURSERY COLLECTION
by Shirley Hughes

Colours, shapes and sizes, sounds, opposites and numbers –
these are the concepts introduced to young children in this delightful nursery picture book
which features a lively toddler and her equally engaging baby brother.

"Predictably first class… Concepts are introduced with domestic examples and Hughes'
characteristic gentle humour." *The Guardian*

0-7445-4378-9   £6.99

Walker Paperbacks are available from most booksellers, or by post from B.B.C.S., P.O. Box 941, Hull, North Humberside HU1 3YQ
24 hour telephone credit card line 01482 224626

To order, send: Title, author, ISBN number and price for each book ordered, your full name and address,
cheque or postal order payable to BBCS for the total amount and allow the following for postage and packing:
UK and BFPO: £1.00 for the first book, and 50p for each additional book to a maximum of £3.50.
Overseas and Eire: £2.00 for the first book, £1.00 for the second and 50p for each additional book.

Prices and availability are subject to change without notice.